IMAGES OF SPORT

ABERDEEN
FOOTBALL CLUB
(1903–1973)

IMAGES OF SPORT

ABERDEEN
FOOTBALL CLUB
(1903–1973)

PAUL LUNNEY

First published in 2000 by
Tempus Publishing

Reprinted in 2009 by
The History Press
The Mill, Brimscombe Port,
Stroud, Gloucestershire, GL5 2QG
www.thehistorypress.co.uk

ISBN 978 0 7524 1860 5

Typesetting and origination by
Tempus Publishing
Printed and bound in Great Britain.

Contents

Acknowledgements

I would like to thank the following for their assistance in making this book possible: Derek Taylor of Kollectables in Glasgow, Jack Murray, Aberdeen Journals Ltd, the *Scottish Daily Express*, David Crotty, Raymond Taylor and everyone at Tempus Publishing, especially their Scottish editor, Matthew Forlow.

Introduction

Aberdeen FC are the third biggest club in Scotland behind the Old Firm of Celtic and Rangers, and yet surprisingly they are one of the country's youngest clubs. Formed in 1903 when the first Aberdeen team amalgamated with Orion and Victoria United, the infant boys from the Granite City were a strong team from the outset.

Jimmy Philip was the first manager of this new version of Aberdeen Football Club and, after a dull 1-1 draw against Stenhousemuir on 15 August 1903, the club's white jerseys were changed to black and gold at the start of the 1904/05 season. Elected to the Scottish Second Division in 1904 and voted into the First Division for the following term, the 'Wasps' lost their first top-flight fixture 1-0 to Partick Thistle on 19 August 1905, but registered a 2-0 win over Kilmarnock a fortnight later. Star performers in the early years included Willie McAuley, Donald Colman, Paddy Travers and Aberdeen's first Scotland international cap, Willie Lennie.

In 1910/11 they began to challenge the Old Firm's dominance of the domestic game in Scotland by losing narrowly 1-0 to Celtic at Parkhead in the Scottish Cup semi-final, and finishing runners-up in the Championship race to Rangers. The First World War put paid to the makings of a fine 'Dons' side and the best the 1920s had to offer was three Scottish Cup semi-final appearances in 1922, 1924 and 1926, without advancement from the penultimate stage of the 'Blue Riband'. The decade did produce two brilliant players, however, in jovial Jock Hutton and future 'Wembley Wizard' Alec Jackson. 1936/37 saw Aberdeen chase the League and Cup 'double', only to lose out at the last hurdle in both competitions, although the club's striking partnership of Matt Armstrong and Willie Mills was the envy of teams the length and breadth of the country.

By the outbreak of the Second World War in 1939, the Dons had still to collect a major honour. The end of hostilities soon rectified this, and in the first official season (1946/47) after the war, Aberdeen defeated Hibernian 2-1 to take the Scottish Cup for the first time in the club's history. David Halliday was now the manager, having taken over from Paddy Travers in 1938, and would remain in the 'hot seat' until his departure to Leicester City in 1955. Scottish Cup failures in 1953 (after a replay) and 1954 were crowned with the Scottish League Division 'A' Championship title in 1954/55.

New boss David Shaw led the team to a League Cup final triumph over St Mirren the following season, but the Paisley 'Buddies' gained revenge in 1959 by beating Aberdeen 3-1 in the Scottish Cup Final. Tommy Pearson's reign as manager from 1959 to 1965 was unsuccessful, with the side sliding down the slippery slope to mediocrity. It also proved a transitional period and saw the brilliant Charlie Cooke make his breakthrough at Pittodrie.

Queen's Park coach Eddie Turnbull took charge in 1965, and his ambition and determination thrust the Dons back into the limelight of Scottish football, the team reaching the final of the country's 'Blue Riband' prize in 1967 and taking the trophy in 1970. Turnbull's Tornadoes also came within a whisker of the League title in 1970/71, although Aberdeen's optimism for the future took a severe blow when the boss decided to join Hibernian in the close season. Jimmy Bonethrone was promoted from coach to manager and won the Drybrough Cup against Celtic almost immediately, but with outstanding players like Martin Buchan and Joe Harper departing south of Hadrain's Wall the club once again went into momentary decline.

This volume is a pictorial account of Aberdeen's first seventy years and is a tribute to star players and major triumphs of yesteryear.

One

Amalgamation and
Early Years
(1903-1920)

Willie McAulay (1903-1906) made 69 League and cup appearances for Aberdeen, scoring 21 goals. An inside left, he joined the club from Middlesbrough in 1903, became the Dons' first skipper and converted their first goal against Stenhousemuir in a 1-1 draw at Pittodrie Park on 15 August 1903. A favourite of the fans, 'Mac' subsequently played at Falkirk and Alloa.

The earliest known photograph of the first Aberdeen FC, taken in 1882.

The team of 1889 show off the impressive Aberdeenshire Cup.

Orion FC in the 1901/02 season.

Victoria United play Orion at Cattofield prior to the 1903 amalgamation.

Two team photographs taken only a season before the three clubs amalgamated.

Aberdeen with the Qualifying Cup after the 1904/05 final in which they beat Renton 2-0 at Dens Park, Dundee.

Jimmy Philip, Aberdeen's manager (1903-1924). He died in Belfast in July 1930 after a car accident.

Aberdeen FC, 1906/07.

Team colours.

Aberdeen FC, 1907/08.

Outside left Willie Lennie (1905-1913) made 251 appearances and scored 67 goals for Aberdeen. A Glaswegian, he began his career with Maryhill FC and played for Queen's Park, Rangers, Dundee and Fulham before signing for the Dons in 1905. A meandering marvel, in March 1908 Lennie became the first Aberdeen player to win a cap for Scotland. He emigrated to the USA after his marriage to an Aberdeen girl.

The Black and Golds of 1908 lost 1-0 to Celtic in their first ever Scottish Cup semi-final at Pittodrie.

Aberdeen FC, 1909/10.

A postcard of the 1910/11 team.

Donald Colman (1907-1920). A legendary figure in the annals of Aberdeen Football Club, he played for Maryhill and Motherwell before moving to Pittodrie in 1907. An excellent right-back, Donald became club captain and won his first full international cap at thirty-three. Appointed Aberdeen's trainer in 1931, he was quite an innovator and was responsible for the introduction of the dugout.

Goalkeeper Andrew Greig (1911-1917) made 80 League and 7 Scottish Cup appearances for Aberdeen.

Forward Jimmy Soye (1905-1915) made 201 appearances and scored 25 goals for Aberdeen. Born in Glasgow on 14 April 1885, he starred for Rutherglen Glencairn, Belfast Celtic, Distillery, Southampton and Newcastle United before joining in May 1909. An electrical engineer by trade, Jimmy's performances at Pittodrie earned him a Scottish League cap in 1912.

Utility player George Wilson (1906-1914) made 197 League and cup appearances for Aberdeen and scored 14 goals. He joined the club in January 1907 from Aberdeen University, giving sterling service until his departure in 1914.

Inside forward Paddy Travers (1910-1914) made 97 League and 7 Scottish Cup appearances for Aberdeen, netting 24 goals in total. Born at Beith on 28 May 1883, he played for a number of clubs, including Thornliebank and Barnsley, before signing for Aberdeen from Clyde in May 1910. Travers moved to Celtic in August 1911 but after an injury curtailed his season he returned to Pittodrie.

Stewart Davidson (1905-1925) made 149 League and cup appearances for Aberdeen, scoring a solitary goal. At 5ft 10in and 11st 10lbs, Stewart was a strong, yet elegant wing-half, who excelled at the precision pass. After a move to Middlesbrough in 1913, he returned to Pittodrie in 1923 having been capped for Scotland against England in 1921.

Aberdeen FC, 1912/13. From left to right, back row: Watson, King, Greig, Milne, Low. Middle row: Hannah, Gault, Main, Hume, Wilson, Walker, McConnell. Front row: Davidson, Edgar, Travers, Lennie, Colman, Soye, Wood, Nelson.

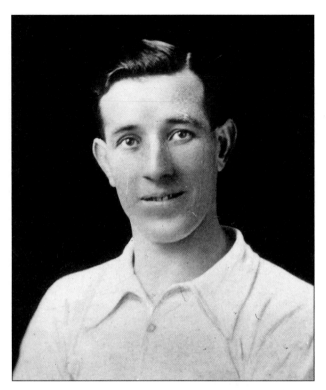

Centre half George 'Dod' Brewster (1912-1920) made 119 League appearances, scoring 9 goals for Aberdeen. The Dons signed him from Mugiemoss and he made his Pittodrie debut in a splendid 3-0 win over Celtic on 15 February 1913. 'Dod' assisted Falkirk during the First World War and cost Everton £1,500 in January 1920. He was capped against England in 1921.

At 6ft and 12st 7lbs, Alec Wright was a formidable force in the Dons half-back line around 1920. He made 143 League and cup appearances, scoring 11 goals for Aberdeen. Wright's service with the 4th Battalion restricted his appearances during the First World War. He received a Scottish League cap in 1922 and was transferred to Hearts for a club record fee of £2,500 in May of the same year.

Two

Jock Hutton and Alex Jackson (1920-1930)

The great Jock Hutton, Aberdeen's burly jovial personality of the 1920s.

Although the caption below his name stated A. Laurie, this is in fact a photograph of George Anderson, Aberdeen's goalkeeper from 1914-1922, who made 213 League and cup appearances for the Dons. Subsequently a successful local businessman and town councillor, he also served the club as director.

Courageous captain and left half Albert 'Al' MacLachlan (1914-1927) made 315 League appearances and scored 16 goals for Aberdeen. A tenacious tackler, Bert was signed from Aston Villa in 1914. He moved to Hearts in September 1927, having also played in 43 Scottish Cup ties for the Dons.

Aberdeen FC, 1921/22.

Defender Bobby Hannah (1910-1922) made 126 League and cup appearances for the Dons. He joined Aberdeen from the local East End side in 1908, but just as his career at Pittodrie had got underway war broke out and he was mobilzed for the 7th Gordon's Batallion. Hannah later emigrated to the USA.

Sandy Grosert (1920-1923) had two spells at Pittodrie, firstly as an amateur and later as a professional after his return from Hibs. Apparently, in his unpaid days at Aberdeen, Sandy had an agreement with manager Jimmy Philip that he should provide him with a bottle of stout after each game. Grosert became a dentist in the city.

Local lad Jacky Connon (1919-1924) made 93 League appearances and scored 22 goals for Aberdeen. He also scored 3 goals in 13 Scottish Cup ties.

Aberdeen FC, 1923/24.

V. E. MILNE.

V.E. Milne was a tall, talented centre half of the early 1920s. Son of the club's chairman Bailie Milne, he attended university and accepted his doctorate on Christmas Eve, 1921.

'Wembley Wizard' Alec Jackson had one season at Pittodrie in 1924/25. In May 1925 he moved to Huddersfield Town for £5,000, and helped the Yorkshire club win the First Division Championship in 1926. The tallest (5ft 10in) of Scotland's tiny forward line which thrashed England 5-1 in 1928, he was dubbed 'The Gay Cavalier' and 'The Flying Scotsman' during his playing days and was capped 17 times for his country. Transferred to Chelsea at a cost of £8,500 in September 1930, Alec Jackson died on 15 November 1946, the result of a road accident while serving in the Army in Egypt. He was only forty-one years old.

F. & J. SMITH'S CIGARETTES

ABERDEEN.

Portrait of John Miller, Aberdeen's prolific goalscorer of the early 1920s.

Harry Blackwell (1921-1930) kept goal for the Dons on 252 occasions. He joined the club from Scunthorpe United in September 1921, and subsequently stood between the posts for Clapton Orient and Preston North End.

Outside left Jimmy Smith (1922-1931) made 336 League and cup appearances for Aberdeen. He arrived at Pittodrie from Rangers in May 1922, and was rarely out of the team for the next nine seasons. Smith moved to Shamrock Rovers in 1931, and then on to Glentoran in 1934.

Aberdeen born and bred, Arthur Robertson (1913-1923) played on 102 occasions for the club.

Douglas Thomson (1920-1923) made 107 appearances and scored 32 goals for the Black and Golds.

Born in Dalziel, Motherwell on 12 March 1897, John Miller (1921-1927) was a member of the family that contributed a quartet of players to Hamilton Accies. Signed from Liverpool in 1921, he made his name as Aberdeen's goalscoring centre forward, with aggregate League and cup figures of 123 matches and 61 goals. Miller also played for Partick Thistle and Clyde.

Robust full-back Jock Hutton (1919-1927) joined Aberdeen as a forward from Bellshill Athletic in April 1919. Like John Miller, he was born in Dalziel, on 29 October 1898. Hutton had a tremendous kick and was surprisingly agile for his size (5ft 9in, 13st 6lbs). Transferred to Blackburn Rovers in October 1926 for £4,000, big Jock won an FA Cup winners medal in 1928 and retired in March 1933. While at Pittodrie, he made 282 League and cup appearances and wore Scotland's dark blue jersey ten times.

Dr Victor E. Milne (1919-1923) was a cultured pivot who spread the ball around well during a game, making 110 League appearances and scoring 3 goals, while his Scottish Cup statistics read 4 goals from 12 starts. Milne joined Aston Villa in 1923 and retained his connection with the Birmingham side by becoming club doctor on his retirement. Vic also played cricket for Aberdeenshire.

The black and golds pose for a photograph as they embark on a tour of South Africa in 1927.

ABERDEEN FOOTBALL CLUB 1928-29

MERRIE, COOPER, DONALD, McHALE, McLAREN, McKENZIE, LEGGE,
RITCHIE, (Asst. Trainer) BLACK, SMITH, JACKSON, BLACKWELL, YUILL, LOVE, McLEOD, LIVINGSTONE, RUSSELL (Trainer)
ROBERTSON (Secretary) POLLAND, WILSON, FALLOON, McDERMID (CAPTAIN) MUIR, YORSTON, CHEYNE, HILL, TRAVERS (MANAGER)
TROPHIES. FLEMING SHIELD = ABERDEENSHIRE COUNTY CUP = ABERDEEN DISTRICT LEAGUE CUP = DEWAR CHALLENGE SHIELD.

The Aberdeen team of 1928/29 show off their silverware. On display are the Fleming Shield, Aberdeenshire Cup, Aberdeen District League Cup, and the Dewar Shield.

Centre half Hugh McLaren (1928–1932) played 105 League and 10 Scottish Cup matches for the Dons. He joined the club from Nithsdale Wanderers in February 1928. Hugh amazingly won a Scottish Cup winners medal while on loan to Kilmarnock in 1929 and left Pittodrie in 1932 to join Workington.

Two portraits of the prolific and brilliant goalscorer Benny Yorston (1927-1932). Born in Nigg on 14 October 1905, Benjamin Collard Yorston starred for Mugiemoss Juniors and Montrose before joining Aberdeen in time for the team's tour of South Africa in 1927. Although small at 5ft 5in (10st 11lbs), Yorston was a quicksilver striker who would outjump huge opponents to score. He played 143 League games and scored 101 goals, amassing a further 24 goals from just 13 Scottish Cup ties. His 38 League goals from 38 starts in 1929/30 is still a club record and, indeed, he registered a total of 46 goals that season by netting 8 more in four Scottish Cup outings. Benny cost Sunderland £2,000 in January 1932 and in March 1934 he signed for Middlesbrough for £1,250. He made guest appearances for a number of English clubs during the Second World War and died in 1977.

Three

Armstrong and Mills
(1930-1940)

Matt Armstrong tries a flying header for Scotland against Wales at Cardiff on 5 October 1935.

Right-back Willie Cooper (1927-1948) was a tremendous servant for Aberdeen. Willie made 373 appearances for the club during his twenty-one years at Pittodrie, a total that no doubt would have passed the 500 mark but for the seven seasons lost to the Second World War. He cost the Dons a fee of £20 in 1927 and was paid £1 a week while he continued to play for his junior team, Mugiemoss. Solid and reliable in defence, he set a new club record of 162 consecutive League appearances. Twice capped by the Scottish League, Cooper joined Huntly as a player/manager in June 1948.

Aberdeen FC, 1932/33.

Aberdeen FC, 1933/34. From left to right, back row: Travers, O'Riley, Cooper, Smith, McGill, Fraser, Thomson, Colman. Front row: Beynon, Beattie, Armstrong, Mills, Gall.

South African Billy Strauss electrified crowds at Pittodrie in the late 1930s with his dazzling wing-play and devastating shooting power.

'Northern lights' inside right McKenzie (left) and captain Bob Fraser (below).

Fine opportunist Matt Armstrong (1931-1939) had a telepathic understanding with Willie Mills at Pittodrie in the 1930s. Born in Newton Stewart on 12 November 1911, Matt was provisionally signed for Celtic from Port Glasgow Juniors. Celtic let him go for free and Aberdeen snapped him up. A prolific scorer in the Alliance team before becoming a regular first-choice striker in 1934, in total Armstrong made 215 League and cup appearances, scoring 155 goals.

Inside left Willie Mills (1932-1938) joined Aberdeen from Bridgeton Waverly in 1932. An accomplished passer of the ball, Willie was also highly skilled and possessed a strong shot. He scored 114 League and cup goals from 210 games, before moving to Huddersfield Town in March 1938 for £6,500. Like team-mate Matt Armstrong, Willie made three appearances in Scotland's dark blue.

Matt Armstrong shows balance and concentration as he fires in a shot.

Poetry in motion – Willie Mills in action.

Clever wing half Bob Fraser (1931-38) made 215 League and Scottish Cup appearances for the club. He arrived at Pittodrie in 1931 from Albion Rovers and became Dons skipper in the mid-1930s. Fraser emigrated to South Africa in 1938 (left).

Full-back Willie Cooper in action (right).

Aberdeen on the receiving end of Jimmy McGrory's head, as the centre breaks the world record for league goals at Parkhead on 21 December 1935.

That's the real Aberdeen spirit, but he might have made a meal of the Dons' shooting-boots. So Beynon picked the pup up and substituted the dummy. Steve Smith appeared to have the wind-up in case Donald Colman would get wind of the prank.

The Mascot – 'Buster'.

Belfast-born Eddie Falloon (1927-1938) joined Aberdeen from Crusaders in the summer of 1927. At 5ft 5in, 10st 6lbs, he was a bulldog type of centre half who could challenge much bigger opponents. Capped by Northern Ireland, Falloon made 249 League and cup outings for the Dons. He later helped Clyde to their Scottish Cup Final win in 1939.

Benoni-born Billy Strauss (1936-1939) was an exciting outside left. Two-footed and with a quick turn of pace, this South African youngster caused havoc in the final third of the field. He made 94 League and cup appearances, scoring 53 goals in the process. Strauss left Aberdeen in 1946 to sign for Plymouth Argyle.

The official matchday programme for the 1937 Scottish Cup final.

Celtic's Canadian 'keeper 'Joe' Kennaway punches clear the danger of an Aberdeen raid during the 1937 Scottish Cup final at Hampden Park.

NORTH STAND ENTER ONLY AT TURNSTILES
(See Plan on back)

D1

Row Q   Seat No. 200

Scottish Cup-Final Tie

HAMPDEN PARK, GLASGOW
Saturday, 24th April, 1937
Kick-off 3 p.m.

Price 5/-   G. G. Graham
(Including Tax)   Secretary

THIS PORTION TO BE RETAINED
(See Conditions on back)

5/-North Stand match ticket for the 1937 Scottish Cup final.

2/6 South Enclosure match ticket for the 1937 Scottish Cup final.

Cartoonist view of the 1937 Scottish Cup Final.

Congratulations and commiserations as the respective club captains Jimmy McGrory (Celtic) and Eddie Falloon (Aberdeen) troop off the pitch at the end of the 1937 Scottish Cup Final. Hampden Park was crammed with 146,433 spectators, still a record for a club match in Europe.

Willie Mills, the Black and Gold's brilliant forward of the 1930s.

Postcards to celebrate the 1938 Empire Exhibition football tournament held at Ibrox Park.

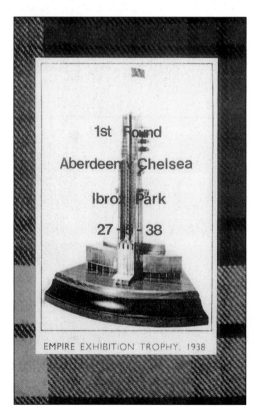

Aberdeen hammered the mighty Chelsea 4-0 in the first round through goals by Strauss, Thomson, Armstrong and Hamilton.

The Dons lost out to Everton 3-2 in the semi-final, having taken a 2-1 lead. Aberdeen's scorers were Armstrong and Strauss.

Aberdeen FC, 1937/38.

Billy Strauss in action.

Four

Hampden Glory
(1940-1950)

Frank Dunlop is presented with the Scottish Cup at Hampden Park after Aberdeen's 2-1 win over Hibernian in 1947.

A 7-3 aggregate victory over Raith Rovers in May 1943 sees Frank Dunlop receive the Mitchell Cup from James Black.

Action shot of inside forward George Hamilton.

Superb all-round footballer George Hamilton (1938-1955) arrived at Pittodrie in April 1938 from Queen of the South. 'Hammy' had boundless enthusiasm and was a joy to watch on the pitch with his skilled footwork. His strict adherence to clean play and the true principles of the game earned him the nickname 'Gentleman George.'

Aberdeen are presented with the Southern League Cup in May 1946 after the team's 3-2 triumph over Rangers before a huge 135,000 crowd at Hampden Park.

The 1947 Scottish Cup Final matchday programme.

South African Stan Williams squeezes the ball between 'keeper Kerr and post to score Aberdeen's winning goal in the 1947 2-1 victory over Hibernian at Hampden Park.

The team let veteran Willie Cooper take centre stage with the Scottish Cup. An injury in the semi-final cost Cooper his Hampden place.

Caricature of Dons legend Willie Cooper.

Hampden hero of the 1947 Scottish Cup Final,
Stan Williams (1938-1949) was born in South
Africa on 1 May 1919.

Long throw-in expert Frank Dunlop (1936-1948) joined the club from Benburb in 1936. Originally a right half, he converted to the centre half berth during the war years and subsequently became club captain. A fine, forcing type of player, Dunlop was a consistent and commanding figure on the pitch. He made 146 League and cup appearances for Aberdeen without scoring a goal.

Tall and strongly built, George Taylor (1933-1948) was born on 9 June 1913 and joined Aberdeen from Hall Russell's in 1937. An excellent left half, he scored the winning goal against Rangers when the Dons won the Southern League Cup in 1946. Taylor made 82 League and cup appearances for the club and netted on 6 occasions. He moved to Plymouth Argyle on 10 August 1948.

JOHNSTONE

Goalkeeper George Johnstone (1936-1949) was a member of Benburb's 1936 Scottish Junior Cup winning side and the following year was at Hampden with Aberdeen in the senior final. He made exactly 200 League and cup appearances for the Dons before being released to Dunfermline Athletic in April 1949. A steady and reliable custodian, 'Big George' had a spell with Celtic during the war, and moved to Raith Rovers in 1950.

Glaswegian Tony Harris (1946-1954) joined Aberdeen from amateurs Queen's Park in 1946. Originally a centre forward, he moved out to the right wing after only a short time as leader of the attack. A cup winner at Pittodrie, Harris was a dentist by profession. He played 273 games for the Dons in a number of positions.

Archie Baird (1938-1953) arrived at Pittodrie from Strathclyde Juniors in 1938. He never got the opportunity to play first-team football before the outbreak of the Second World War and found himself a POW in Italy. However, Archie was back playing for the Dons in March 1945. A PT instructor away from the game, as a classy inside left he was unfortunately injury prone. Capped by Scotland in an unofficial wartime international, Baird made 144 League and cup appearances for Aberdeen before being released to St Johnstone in 1953.

KIDDIE

Outside left Alex Kiddie (1945-1950) was born in Dundee on 27 April 1927. He made a couple of wartime appearances for Celtic before Aberdeen signed him in August 1945. Alex was a very fast wingman with a deceptive swerve and always quick to seize an opportunity. A university student, he acquired a BSc degree at St Andrew's in 1948, and secured his future outside football as a schoolteacher at St John's, Dundee. He played 48 League and cup games for the Dons, netting 13 goals.

The Southern League Cup and match ball go on display in the *Evening Express* window.

Aberdeen players and officials are proudly photographed with the Scottish Cup in 1947.

Five

Champions and Scottish Cup Blues (1950-1960)

The Aberdeen team which captured the Scottish League Division 'A' Championship in 1955. From left to right, back row: Paterson, Caldwell, Martin O'Neil, Young, Glen. Front row: Leggat, Yorston, Buckley, Wishart, Hather.

Jimmy Delaney (1950-1952) established a unique record by winning national cup winners' medals in England, Scotland and Northern Ireland, and almost made it a quartet (he was a losing finalist in Eire). Jimmy made his name with Celtic and joined Aberdeen from Manchester United for £3,000 in November 1950. Outside right Delaney played in 39 League and cup games for the Dons and scored 11 goals. He is perhaps best remembered for his last minute winner in the 1946 Scotland England fixture at Hampden Park.

Although Paddy Buckley had already signed for Celtic, the SFA ordered him to remain at St Johnstone in 1948. A small, speedy centre forward, Buckley was in the Joe Harper mould and joined Aberdeen from the 'Saints' in April 1952 for £7,500. He made 152 League and cup appearances for the Dons and scored 92 goals. Paddy retired through injury in 1957, but subsequently had a spell with Inverness Caledonian.

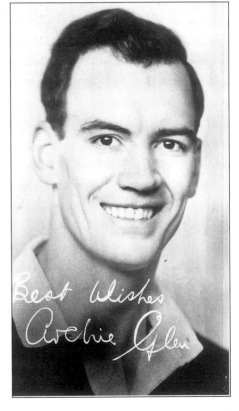

Born at Coalburn on 16 April 1929, Archie Glen (1947-1960) was a wing half of quality, being skilled in the arts of his position, particularly the well-timed tackle. He joined the Dons from Annbank United in 1947, but his early career at Pittodrie was restricted by National Service. Capped by Scotland on two occasions, Glen made 269 League and cup appearances for Aberdeen and scored 27 goals. He maintained an excellent level of performance and captained the club just after their purple patch in the mid-1950s.

Forward Tommy Bogan (1951-1952) must have the shortest international career on record. For the 1945 Scotland England match at Hampden, he was injured within a minute of the kick-off, had to leave the field and was unable to resume. He joined Aberdeen from Manchester United in March 1952 and departed to Southampton in December 1952, having made just 9 League and cup appearances and scoring 1 goal. Employed in the newspaper industry, Bogan married Sir Matt Busby's neice.

Born at Cleland on 3 September 1914, Jimmy Delaney was a magical winger with dazzling speed and dribbling ability. On leaving Pittodrie in December 1951, Jimmy joined Falkirk and ended his playing career at Elgin City in 1957. He died in September 1989, aged 75.

Aberdeen's official matchday programme for the visit of Celtic on Saturday 29 December 1957. The fixture finished 4-3 in Celtic's favour. In a furious climax to the game, Emery scored a penalty after 82 minutes and Yorston netted in the last minute, but the Dons left it too late to salvage a share of the points.

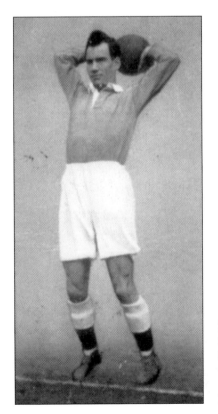

Skipper Archie Glen takes a throw-in. Glen played football for the British Army during his National Service and won a host of honours with Aberdeen in the 1950s. These included a Championship medal in 1954/55, the League Cup in 1955/56 and six Scottish League caps.

Official matchday programme for the 1953 Scottish Cup Final at Hampden Park. The result was a 1-1 draw.

Harry Yorston nets Aberdeen's late equalizer in the 1953 Scottish Cup Final against Rangers. The Ibrox club won the replay 1-0.

Fred Martin (1949-1960) made 291 League and cup appearances between the posts at Aberdeen. Born at Carnoustie, Angus on 13 May 1929, Fred joined the Dons from Carnoustie Panmure in 1946 as an inside forward, and was converted to goalkeeper when on national service, during which time he played for the British Army. A mainstay of the great side of the mid-1950s, Martin could anticipate situations and showed excellent judgement.

Dons small and stocky striker Paddy Buckley in action against Celtic at Parkhead in the 1950s.

Archie Glen leads out the Scotland 'B' team at Dens Park, Dundee on 29 February 1956 for the international against England 'B'. The match ended in a 2-2 draw.

The official programme for the Dons 1954 Scottish Cup semi-final against Rangers at Hampden Park. Aberdeen thrashed the Glasgow giants 6-0, Joe O'Neil scoring a hat-trick with Leggat, Allister and Buckley providing the other goals.

The match programme for the 1954 Final against Celtic. Paddy Buckley scored the Dons goal in the 2-1 defeat.

Sean Fallon scores Celtic's winner in the 1954 Scottish Cup Final. The parkhead club's other goal came from an unfortunate own goal by Young when he tried a clearance and sliced the ball past Martin.

The men who helped Aberdeen carry off the Scottish 'A' League Championship for the first time in 1954/55. From left to right, back row: Shaw (Trainer), Mitchell, Caldwell, Martin, Allister, Young, Glen. Front row: Leggat, Hamilton, Yorston, Buckley, Wishart, O'Neil, Hather. Insets: Halliday (Manager) and Smith.

The 1954/55 Scottish League Division 'A' Championship Flag flies over Pittodrie.

Aberdeen FC, 1954/55. From left to right, back row: Paterson, Caldwell, Martin, O'Neil, Young, Glen. Front row: Leggat, Yorston, Buckley, Wishart, Hather.

The 1954/55 League Championship squad. From left to right, back row: Hather, Glen, Smith, O'Neil, Morrison, Martin, Wishart, Allister, Wallace, Caldwell, Leggat. Front row: Robbie, Mitchell, Brown, Paterson, Buckley, Mitchell, Young, Yorston, Hamilton, Forbes, Halliday.

A 1954/55 League Championship medal.

The match programme for the 1955/56 League Cup semi-final between Aberdeen and Rangers. The Dons won 2-1 through goals by Laggat and Wishart.

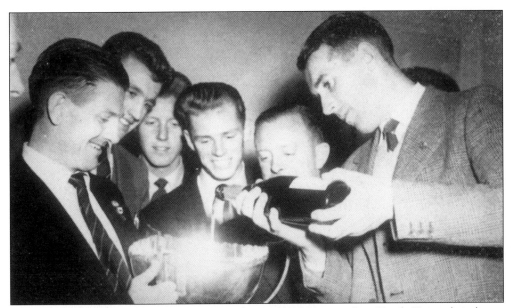

Aberdeen defeated St Mirren 2-1 to win the 1955/56 League Cup Final. Here, the players celebrate by pouring champagne into the trophy.

The excellent opportunist Graham Leggat (1953-1958) played in all five forward positions but was at his best at outside-right. Very skillful and a noted goal-poacher, Leggat hit 92 goals in 151 League and Cup appearances for Aberdeen. He joined the club from Banks o'Dee in 1953, and became a regular choice for Aberdeen and Scotland. Graham was transferred to Fulham for £16,000 in August 1958, subsequently starring for Birmingham City before retiring.

Profile and action shot of Graham Leggat as portrayed by the football artist.

Aberdeen FC, 1956/57.

The Dons on the defensive during a League fixture against Clyde at Shawfield Stadium in 1958.

Fred Martin was capped six times for Scotland and made a further three appearances for the Scottish League in the 1950s.

Ball-playing inside left Bob Wishart (1953-1961) joined Aberdeen from Mechiston Thistle in 1952. A key member of the successful Dons side of the 1950s, Wishart represented Scotland at Under-23 level and was capped twice by the Scottish League. He made 236 League and cup appearances and scored 62 goals.

Centre forward Hugh Baird (1958-1962) made 86 League and cup appearances for the Dons, netting 25 goals. Born at Calderbank on 14 March 1930, he cost Aberdeen £11,000 from Leeds United in October 1958. Baird began his career at Dalry Thistle and moved to Airdrieonians in March 1951. Whilst at Broomfield, he won a 'B' Division Championship medal in 1955, and was capped for Scotland the following year against Austria.

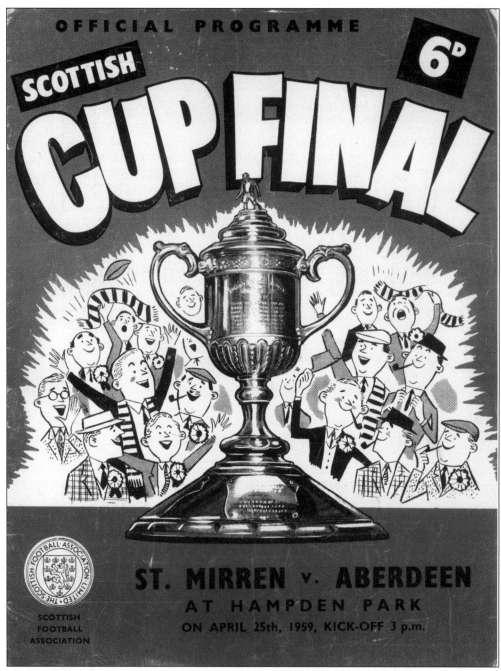

The 1959 Scottish Cup Final match programme.

St Mirren gained revenge for their 1955/56 League Cup Final defeat by beating Aberdeen 3-1 in the 1959 Scottish Cup Final.

Goalkeeper Fred Martin feels the strain as Saints pile on the pressure.

An aerial view of Pittodrie Park in the 1950s.

Fred Martin in action against Hearts at Tynecastle Park.

84

Six

Mediocrity and Transition
(1960-1965)

Aberdeen FC, 1961/62. From left to right, back row: Burns, Coutts, Fraser, Ogston, Caldenhead, Baird. Front row: Cummings, Little, Hogg, Cooke, Mulhall.

Whether as winger or inside forward Charlie Cooke (1959-1965), was a handful for any defence. Douglas Lamming summed him up perfectly when he wrote, 'One of the most brilliant dribbling and ball control talents to emerge in recent times: a twisting, feinting, tantalising forward with tremendous entertainment value.' Cooke joined Aberdeen from Renfrew Juniors in October 1959 and made 165 League and cup appearances for the club before moving to Dundee for a Scottish transfer fee of £44,000 in December 1964. He cost Chelsea £72,000 in April 1966 and Crystal Palace £85,000 mid-way through the 1972/73 season. Charlie later coached in the USA.

An Aberdeen attack at Parkhead from Dick Ewen, and Billy Little is foiled by Celtic goalkeeper John Fallon.

This time Dons 'keeper John 'Tubby' Ogston is brought into the action against Celtic at Parkhead.

Custodian Ogston saves a penalty from Dundee's Andy Penman at Dens Park in the early 1960s.

Ogston collects the ball in the same game, but it's too late, Dundee have already scored against the Dons.

'Tubby' Ogston saves from Celtic's centre-forward Jim Conway.

Aberdeen FC, 1962/63. From left to right, back row: Bennett, Ewen, Smith, Allan, Caldenhead, Little. Middle row: Winchester, Will, Burns, Fraser, Law, Thomson, Ogston, Hogg, Anderson, McMilllan, Coutts, Shewan, Brownlee. Front row: Cummings, Turnbull, Lewis, Donald, Kinnell, Wilson, Cooke, Callaghan, Mulhall.

An artistic postcard of a Scotland supporter shouting for his team in a match against Aberdeen.

Aberdeen FC, 1964/65. From left to right, back row: Bennett, Shewan, Ogston, Cooke, Smith, Kerr. Front row: Kerrigan, Morrison, Coutts, Winchester, McIntosh.

Seven

Turnbull's Tornadoes (1965-1971)

Dons' Danish trio from left to right: Lief Mortensen, Jorgen Ravn and Jens Petersen.

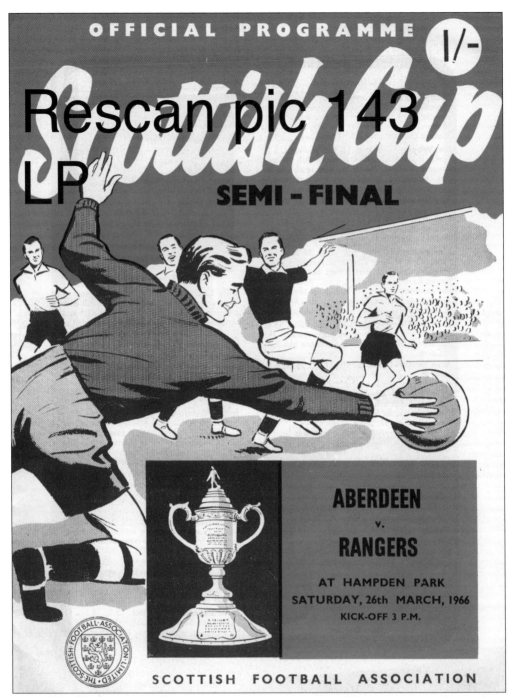

Match programme for the 1966 Scottish Cup Semi-final against Rangers at Hampden Park.

Aberdeen went 'this close' to a place in the 1966 Scottish Cup Final. Ravn beat Rangers 'keeper Ritchie with this shot that hit the post. Winchester followed up but somehow managed to put the ball wide of the goal. Rangers won the replay 2-1.

Aberdeen FC, 1965/66. From left to right, back row: Ravn, Winchester, Bennett, Ogston, McCormack, Smith. Front row: Little, Millar, Shewan, White, Wilson.

Soccer wizard Jimmy 'Jinky' Smith (1965-1969) demonstrates the volley. Glaswegian Smith joined the Dons from Benburb in 1965 and moved to Newcastle United in the summer of 1969 for an estimated £80,000 sum. He made 140 League and cup appearances while at Pittodrie, and scored 37 goals. Jimmy Smith retired through injury in 1976 but was able to have a spell with Whitley Bay in 1977 as a permit player. A class act.

Aberdeen FC, 1966. From left to right, back row: Whyte, McMillan, Clark, Petersen, Winchester, D. Smith. Front row: Little, Melrose, Shewan, J. Smith, Wilson.

Aberdeen FC, 1967. From left to right, back row: Whyte, Munro, Clark, McMillan, Petersen, Shewan. Front row: Little, Smith, Johnston, Melrose, Wilson.

Aberdeen's Bobby Clark and Jim Whyte on the defensive against Rangers at Ibrox in the 1966/67 season.

Bobby Clark catches a high ball and avoids Celtic captain Billy McNeil's challenge during a clash at Parkhead in 1967.

Bobby Clark holds the ball despite a challenge from Dundee United's Scandanavian forwards, Dossing and Wing. Dons won this 1967 Scottish Cup semi-final at Dens Park thanks to an own goal by Tommy Millar after only three minutes.

A caricature of Jimmy Smith.

The official matchday programme for the 1967 Scottish Cup final.

An aerial view of Hampden Park, *c.* 1967. Notice Cathkin Park, home of Third Lanark FC, in the top left hand corner of the photograph.

Captains Harry Melrose (Aberdeen) and Billy McNeil (Celtic) lead out their teams for the Scottish Cup final at Hampden Park in April 1967.

Dons defenders Frank Munro and Jim Whyte stop Celtic's Bobby Lennox in his tracks during the 1967 Scottish Cup final at Hampden Park. Celtic won 2-0 thanks to goals either side of the interval from Willie Wallace.

An amazing escape for Celtic during the 1967 final at Hampden. Aberdeen's Jim Storrie looked certain to score but 'keeper Ronnie Simpson somehow managed to make a goal line clearance for the Celts.

Aberdeen's first taste of competitive European football was in the Cup Winners Cup in 1967/68. They defeated Reykjavik of Iceland 14-1 on aggregate, but lost 3-2 to Standard Leige in the second round.

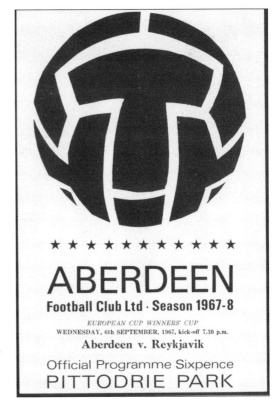

★ ★ ★ ★ ★ ★ ★ ★ ★ ★ ★ ★

ABERDEEN

Football Club Ltd · Season 1967-8

EUROPEAN CUP WINNERS' CUP
WEDNESDAY, 6th SEPTEMBER, 1967, kick-off 7.30 p.m.

Aberdeen v. Reykjavik

Official Programme Sixpence
PITTODRIE PARK

The Dons go behind after only two minutes to this wonder strike from Celtic youngster George Connelly at Parkhead in 1968.

Jim Whyte in a tussle for the ball with Kilmarnock's McIlroy in the 1968/69 season.

Official programme for the 1969 Scottish Cup semi-final.

A goal line clearance from right back Jim Whyte during the 1969 Scottish Cup semi-final against Rangers at Celtic Park. The Ibrox side gained some revenge for their 6-0 revenge in the 1954 semi-final by defeating the Dons 6-1.

Striker Jim Forrest fires in a shot against Morton at Cappielow in 1968/69.

The official programme for the 1970 Scottish Cup Semi-final.

Derek McKay scores the only goal of the 1970 semi-final encounter against Kilmarnock at Muirton Park, Perth.

Match ticket for the
1970 Scottish Cup final.

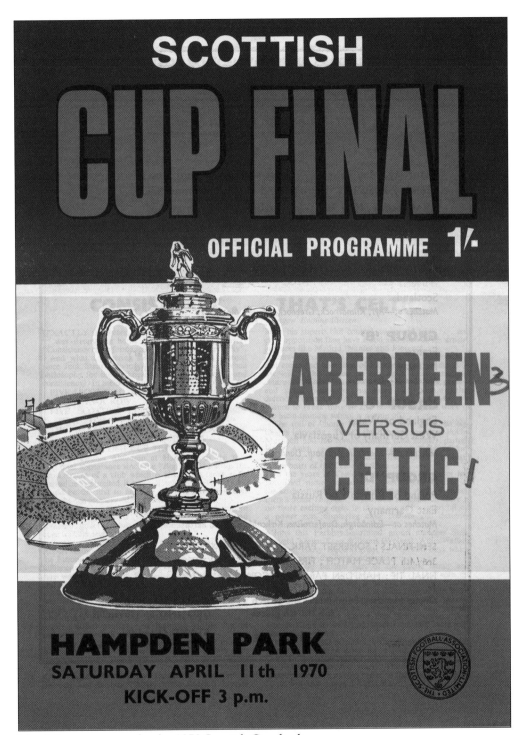

Matchday programme for the 1970 Scottish Cup final.

In the thick of the action, Martin Buchan tackles Celtic's Willie Wallace in the 1970 Scottish Cup final at Hampden Park. Aberdeen won 3-1 to lift the trophy for only the second time in their history.

Aberdeen full back Jim Hermiston keeps Celts' Bobby Lennox in check during the 1970 final.

Bobby Clark saves from Billy McNeil as McMillan and Robb look on with worry etched on their faces.

Derek McKay wraps up the
Dons 1970 victory with the
third goal.

Captain Martin Buchan raises the Scottish Cup
above his head to the fans, acclaim after the famous
1970 3-1 win over Celtic.

Martin Buchan and manager Eddie Turnbull show off the Cup to fans and press outside the national stadium.

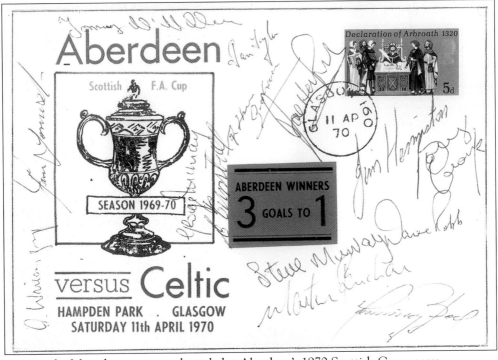

Autographed first day cover to acknowledge Aberdeen's 1970 Scottish Cup success.

Striker David Robb ploughs through the mud and rain in a League encounter against Hearts at Tynecastle Park.

Captain Martin Buchan controls the play during a game at Ibrox Stadium against Rangers.

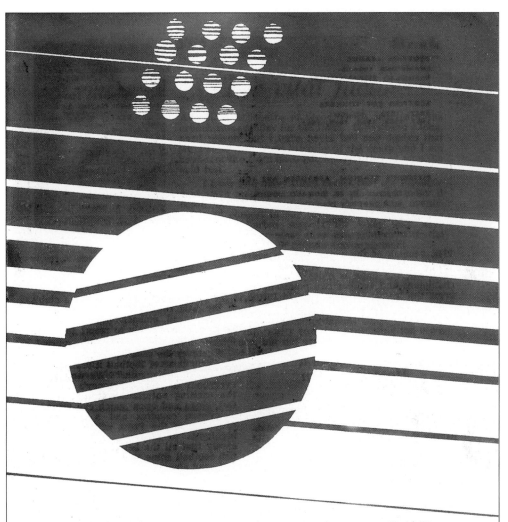

ABERDEEN

Football Club Ltd.   Season 1970-71

SCOTTISH LEAGUE

Aberdeen v. Celtic

SATURDAY, 17th APRIL, 1971, kick-off 3 p.m.

Official Programme - - 1/-

PITTODRIE STADIUM

Programme cover for Aberdeen's 1970/71 Championship decider against Celtic at Pittodrie.

THE " match of the season " is an overworked description, but for once it really can be applied in terms of the league championship to today's encounter. For the Dons, the issue is quite straightforward — victory today over the defending champions and another two points in their last game of the season at Falkirk will bring the league championship to Pittodrie for only the second time in the club's 68-year history. A draw today could mean the title remaining in Celtic's hands for a sixth successive year, but the men from Parkhead, ambassadors of attacking football, are unlikely to resort to defensive tactics to achieve this end.

✦ ✦

Message from Celtic Manager

" THE SUCCESS of Aberdeen in establishing themselves as a threat to the Old Firm has been a boost to the game, and, no doubt, a joy to all their fans. However, we don't intend to give up our title as champions easily. If, however, we do, I can see no club more worthy of being champions than the Dons, and if not this year, perhaps the experience of this season, plus the added support of the Aberdeen fans, will drive them on next season.

" Today we look forward to a good, exciting, sporting game, and one in which the fans of both sides will get their money's worth."

—JOCK STEIN.

Whatever the result today, let us hope that as a game of football it really is the " match of the season." We would like everybody to get their money's worth in the exciting entertainment that only a fast, clean and open match can provide. Television cameras and a formidable gathering of the Press will convey the highlights to millions. We hope sincerely that all the best features in Scottish football shine through for all to see and read about.

TAKE CARE

SPECTATORS ARE REQUESTED NOT TO RUN IN ANY SECTION OF PITTODRIE STADIUM AND TO REFRAIN ESPECIALLY FROM RUNNING OR HURRYING AT THE END OF THE MATCH. IT WILL BE IN THE INTERESTS OF EVERYONE TO MOVE TO THE EXITS IN AN ORDERLY, UNHURRIED MANNER.

NEXT MATCHES AT PITTODRIE STADIUM

CHALLENGE MATCH	RESERVE LEAGUE
Eintracht Brunswick	**Falkirk A**
Monday, April 19	Saturday, April 24
KICK-OFF 7.30 p.m.	KICK-OFF 3 p.m.

Programme notes – a message from Celtic manager Jock Stein before the important league title clash in 1971.

The vital factor

AFTER nine months of blood, sweat and tears, the crunch comes today for the Dons. It has been a long, hard season, but I have never had any doubts that we would be in their pitching at the death and I am confident the team have got what it takes to pass the acid test.

I have said many times before that the Pittodrie fans have an important role to play, and today it could be the vital factor in tipping an evenly-balanced contest in our favour. The Dons deserve your wholehearted support for what they **have** achieved and for what they **can** achieve with the inspiration of your 90-minute encouragement.

The stage is set for a classic encounter. Both teams have got where they are with attacking football. Add the championship incentive and the atmosphere of a "full house" and we, the spectators, can sit back in expectation. But for the players this is the moment for the supreme effort. We have presented Celtic with different problems the last three times we have met—problems which they have failed to solve. Gone are the days of an inferiority complex presenting too big a burden. The players are full of confidence, but not arrogance. They know that past results count for nothing today. The Dons will have to go out again to prove that they are a better team than the title-holders. If they do that, they will be worthy champions themselves.

—EDDIE TURNBULL.

Programme notes – Dons boss Eddie Turnbull's viewpoint before the vital 1971 clash with Celtic.

Aberdeen F.C. Fixtures, 1970-71

SCOTTISH LEAGUE CUP

	Goals—	F	A	Pt	Scorers
Aug. 8—Airdrie ....a		1	1	1	S. Murray
„ 12—St. Johnstone ...h		2	1	2	Harper, Robb
„ 15—Hibs ....h		1	1	1	Robb
„ 19—St. Johnstone ...a		1	0	2	Forrest
„ 22—Airdrie ....h		7	3	2	Harper 4 (1 pen.), Robb, Boel. Jonquin (o.g.)
„ 26—Hibs ....a		0	4	0	

EUROPEAN CUP-WINNERS CUP

Sept. 16—Honved ....h		3	1		Graham, Harper, S. Murray
„ 30—Honved ....a		1	3		S. Murray

CHALLENGE MATCH

Nov. 25—Gornik Zabrze ...h		5	0		Graham, Robb, S. Murray, Hermiston, Forrest
Mar. 30—Coventry City ...a		0	1		

SCOTTISH LEAGUE

Aug. 29—Airdrie ....h		1	1	1	Harper
Sept. 5—Dundee ....a		2	1	2	Harper, Hamilton
„ 12—St. Johnstone ...h		0	0	1	
„ 19—Kilmarnock ......a		4	0	2	Hamilton, Harper, Boel, Arthur (o.g.)
„ 26—Hibs ....h		3	0	2	Forrest, Robb, Harper
Oct. 3—Morton ....a		0	2	0	
„ 10—Dunfermline ......h		3	2	2	Graham 2, M. Buchan
„ 17—Rangers ....a		2	0	2	Jackson (o.g.), Harper
„ 24—St. Mirren ......a		3	1	2	Robb, S. Murray, Forrest
„ 31—Dundee Utd. ......h		4	0	2	Robb, S. Murray, Harper 2
Nov. 7—Clyde ....h		3	0	2	Harper 2, Hermiston
„ 14—Ayr Utd. ....a		1	0	2	Harper
„ 21—Hearts ....h		1	0	2	Harper (penalty)
„ 28—Motherwell ......a		2	0	2	Boel, Taylor
Dec. 5—Cowdenbeath ......h		7	0	2	Harper 3, Graham, S. Murray, Kinnell 2 o.g.
„ 12—Celtic ....a		1	0	2	Harper
„ 19—Falkirk ....h		1	0	2	Harper (penalty)
„ 26—Airdrie ....a		4	0	2	Taylor, S. Murray, Harper 2
Jan. 1—Dundee ....h		3	0	2	McMillan, S. Murray, Graham
„ 2—St. Johnstone ...a		1	0	2	Forrest
„ 9—Kilmarnock ......h		3	0	2	Robb, Forrest, Willoughby
„ 16—Hibs ....a		1	2	0	Robb
„ 30—Morton ....h		3	1	2	Harper, Taylor 2
Feb. 6—Dunfermline ......a		0	1	0	
„ 20—Rangers ....h		0	0	1	
„ 27—St. Mirren ....h		1	1	1	Forrest
Mar. 10—Dundee Utd. ......a		2	0	2	M. Buchan, Forrest
„ 13—Clyde ....a		2	1	2	Graham, Forrest
„ 24—Ayr Utd. ....h		4	1	2	Robb, Graham, Forrest, S. Murray
„ 27—Hearts ....a		3	1	2	Robb 3
Apl. 3—Motherwell ......h		0	0	1	
„ 10—Cowdenbeath ...a		2	1	2	Bostock (o.g.), G. Buchan
„ 17—Celtic ....h					
„ 24—Falkirk ....a					

SCOTTISH CUP

Jan. 25—Elgin City ....h		5	0		Taylor, Forrest 2, Harper 2
Feb. 13—Dundee Utd. ......a		1	1		Forrest
„ 17—Dundee Utd. ......h		2	0		Boel, Robb
Mar. 6—Rangers ....a		0	1		

Programme notes – Aberdeen's games and goalscorers for the 1970/71 season. Unfortunately, the Dons drew 1-1 with Celtic and lost 1-0 to Falkirk to give the Glasgow club the title.

116

THE TABLE-TOPPING DONS

The 17 Dons who have played in league matches this season.

Programme notes – The Aberdeen player pool for 1970/71.

Three Dons' wins in

JOE HARPER scores from the penalty spot in last season's Scottish Cup final against Celtic.

IT MUST be many years—if ever—since a provincial team registered three successive victories over Celtic in Glasgow, but that's the Dons' proud record over the past 12 months. A league win at Parkhead on March 27 last year set Mr. Turnbull's men up for the Scottish Cup final triumph, and last December th Dons leapfrogged over Celts to the top of the table by winning again at Parkhead.

The teams for the Parkhead encounter just over 12 months ago were:

CELTIC — Williams; Craig, Gemmell; Murdoch, McNeill, Brogan; Johnstone, Connelly, Wallace, Lennox, Auld.

ABERDEEN — Clark; Boel, G. Murray; S. Murray, McMillan, M. Buchan; McKay, Hermiston, Robb, Willoughby, Graham.

George Murray opened the scoring in the 49th minute and Arthur Graham made it 2-0 for the Dons with a header in 65 minutes. Tommy Gemmell got one back for Celtic three minutes from time, but it was too late to prevent the Dons scoring their first win over the Parkhead club in 13 matches. It was also the Dons' first win at Parkhead since season 1962-63.

That shock victory which delayed Celtic's league championship celebrations did not stop the bookmakers making the Celts overwhelming favourites when the teams met again in the cup final on April 11. But the Dons confounded the West of Scotland pundits again with a magnificent 3-1 triumph.

The teams at Hampden Park were:

ABERDEEN — Clark; Boel. G. Murray. Hermiston, McMillan. M. Buchan; McKay, Robb, Forrest, Harper, Graham. Sub—G. Buchan.

CELTIC—Williams; Hay, Gemmell; Murdoch, McNeill, Brogan; Johnstone, Wallace, Connelly, Lennox, Hughes (Auld).

Aberdeen went ahead with a controversial penalty kick by Joe Harper in 27 minutes and Derek McKay made it 2-0 in the 83rd minute. Bobby Lennox raised the hopes of the Celtic fans in the 108,434 crowd by reducing the leeway in the 88th minute, but McKay quickly crushed them again with a third goal for the Dons in the next minute.

Game to the last, the bookmakers again installed Celtic as favourites to put a damper on the Dons' title challenge in the league game at Celtic Park on December 12 when the teams were:

CELTIC—Fallon; Craig, Gemmell; Murdoch McNeill, Brogan; Johnstone, Connelly (Hood), Macari, Hay, Hughes.

ABERDEEN — Clark; Boel, Hermiston; S. Murray, McMillan, M. Buchan; Taylor, Robb, Forrest, Harper, Graham.

A hard-fought battle was won for the Dons in the 53rd minute when Dave Robb headed on a long throw-in by Jim Hermiston and Joe Harper was waiting in the middle to head the ball into the net past keeper Fallon.

Lest the Dons' supporters get carried away with their favourites' triple success, it should now be pointed out that Pittodrie holds no fears for Celtic, who have not lost on a trip to Aberdeen for more than five years.

The last time the Dons won a home game against them was on January 15, 1966, when Celtic slipped to a 3-1 defeat on a snow-covered Pittodrie. The teams that day were:

ABERDEEN — Clark; Shewan, McCormick; Petersen, McMillan, D. Smith; Little, Melrose, Winchester, Ravn, J. Wilson.

CELTIC—Simpson; Craig, Gemmell; Murdoch, Cushley, Clark; Johnstone, Gallagher, McBride, Chalmers, Hughes.

Joergen Ravn equalised an early counter by Joe McBride and Ernie Winchester and Billy Little got the goals which ended a Celtic run of 24 games without defeat.

The overall tally in post-war Aberdeen v. Celtic league games is: Celtic 23 wins; Aberdeen 16 wins; draws 11; Celtic 96 goals, Aberdeen 70. Breaking that down to Pittodrie post-war league clashes reveals that honours are almost exactly even—Aberdeen 10 wins; Celtic 11 wins; 4 draws; Aberdeen 41 goals, Celtic 41 goals.

Programme notes – Previous Aberdeen Celtic fixtures.

118

POST-WAR CLASHES

1945-46	ABERDEEN 1, CELTIC ... 1	CELTIC ... 1, ABERDEEN 1
1946-47	ABERDEEN 6, CELTIC ... 2	CELTIC ... 1, ABERDEEN 5
1947-48	ABERDEEN 2, CELTIC ... 0	CELTIC ... 1, ABERDEEN 1
1948-49	ABERDEEN 1, CELTIC ... 0	CELTIC ... 3, ABERDEEN 0
1949-50	ABERDEEN 4, CELTIC ... 0	CELTIC ... 2, ABERDEEN 4
1950-51	ABERDEEN 2, CELTIC ... 1	CELTIC ... 3, ABERDEEN 4
1951-52	ABERDEEN 3, CELTIC ... 4	CELTIC ... 2, ABERDEEN 0
1952-53	ABERDEEN 2, CELTIC ... 2	CELTIC ... 1, ABERDEEN 3
1953-54	ABERDEEN 2, CELTIC ... 0	CELTIC ... 3, ABERDEEN 0
1954-55	ABERDEEN 0, CELTIC ... 2	CELTIC ... 2, ABERDEEN 1
1955-56	ABERDEEN 1, CELTIC ... 0	CELTIC ... 1, ABERDEEN 1
1956-57	ABERDEEN 1, CELTIC ... 2	CELTIC ... 2, ABERDEEN 1
1957-58	ABERDEEN 0, CELTIC ... 1	CELTIC ... 1, ABERDEEN 1
1958-59	ABERDEEN 3, CELTIC ... 1	CELTIC ... 4, ABERDEEN 0
1959-60	ABERDEEN 3, CELTIC ... 2	CELTIC ... 1, ABERDEEN 1
1960-61	ABERDEEN 1, CELTIC ... 3	CELTIC ... 0, ABERDEEN 0
1961-62	ABERDEEN 0, CELTIC ... 0	CELTIC ... 2, ABERDEEN 0
1962-63	ABERDEEN 1, CELTIC ... 5	CELTIC ... 1, ABERDEEN 2
1963-64	ABERDEEN 0, CELTIC ... 3	CELTIC ... 3, ABERDEEN 0
1964-65	ABERDEEN 1, CELTIC ... 3	CELTIC ... 8, ABERDEEN 0
1965-66	ABERDEEN 3, CELTIC ... 1	CELTIC ... 7, ABERDEEN 1
1966-67	ABERDEEN 1, CELTIC ... 1	CELTIC ... 0, ABERDEEN 0
1967-68	ABERDEEN 0, CELTIC ... 1	CELTIC ... 4, ABERDEEN 1
1968-69	ABERDEEN 1, CELTIC ... 3	CELTIC ... 2, ABERDEEN 1
1969-70	ABERDEEN 2, CELTIC ... 3	CELTIC ... 1, ABERDEEN 2
1970-71	CELTIC ... 0, ABERDEEN 1	

SCOTTISH CUP

1950	CELTIC ... 0, ABERDEEN 1
1951	CELTIC ... 3, ABERDEEN 0
1954	ABERDEEN 1, CELTIC ... 2
1967	ABERDEEN 0, CELTIC ... 2
1970	ABERDEEN 3, CELTIC ... 1

LEAGUE CUP

1949-50	ABERDEEN 4, CELTIC ... 5	CELTIC ... 1, ABERDEEN 3
1953-54	ABERDEEN 5, CELTIC ... 2	CELTIC ... 0, ABERDEEN 1
1956-57	ABERDEEN 1, CELTIC ... 2	CELTIC ... 3, ABERDEEN 2
1967-68	ABERDEEN 1, CELTIC ... 5	CELTIC ... 3, ABERDEEN 1
1969-70	ABERDEEN 0, CELTIC ... 0	CELTIC ... 2, ABERDEEN 1

Programme notes – Previous Aberdeen Celtic fixtures.

The 1970/71 Aberdeen squad that came so close to winning the League title. From left to right, back row: Whyte, S. Murray, Hermiston, Boel, Clark, McMillan, M. Buchan, G. Murray, Robb. Front row: McKay, Harper, Willoughby, Turnbull (Manager), Forrest, G. Buchan, Hamilton, Graham.

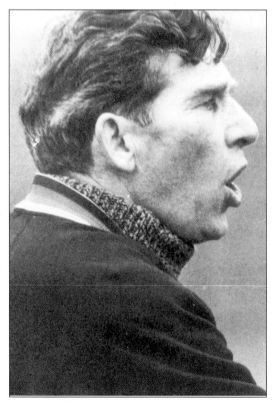

The man who made it possible for Aberdeen to challenge Celtic for Scotland's honours – Eddie Turnbull. Born in 1923 in Falkirk, Eddie joined Hibs at the end of the Second World War, becoming an integral part of their famous five line-up of the era. A highly competitive inside forward noted for his ferocious shot, Eddie won honours for club and country before taking up the post of trainer at Easter Road in 1959. In March 1963, he became coach of Queen's Park and two years later succeeded Tommy Pearson as Aberdeen manager. Turnbull guided the Dons to the 1967 Scottish Cup Final at Hampden, but missed the big day due to illness. Three years later, in 1970, his presence was felt as Aberdeen gained revenge by defeating Celtic 3-1 in the final. After missing out on the League title by a whisker in 1970/71, Eddie moved back to his spiritual home at Easter Road, and as the Dons declined, Hibs jumped out to become Scotland's number two team behind Celtic.

Eight

Bonethrone Takes Over (1971-1973)

Aberdeen coach Jimmy Bonethrone was appointed manager at Pittodrie on Turnbull's departure in the summer of 1971. He had barely taken the 'hot seat' when the Dons defeated Celtic 2-1 in the inaugural Drybrough Cup final. Bonethrone played for East Fife in the 1950s and later became manager of the club. He resigned as Aberdeen boss in October 1975.

Captain Martin Buchan triumphantly raises the Drybrough Cup at Pittodrie after Aberdeen's success over Celtic.

The Drybrough Cup winners of 1971/72. (From left to right, back row: McMillan, Hermiston, Boel, Georghan, Clark, Young, Robb. Front row: G. Buchan, Harper, M. Buchan, Manager Bonethrone, Willoughby, Graham, Murray.)

The Dons' Davie Robb and Willie Young on the attack aginst Airdrieonians at Pittodrie Stadium.

Born in Aberdeen on 6 March 1949, sweeper Martin Buchan (1966-1972) played 192 competitive games for Dons before joining Manchester United for a club record of £125,000 in February 1972. The only Scotsman to captain both Scottish Cup (1970) and FA Cup (1977) winning teams, he was capped on thirty-two occasions for his country, and was also voted Scotland's 'Player of the Year' in 1971.

Celtic captain Billy McNeil puts the ball in his own goal to give Aberdeen a 1-1 draw at Parkhead in November 1971. Dons midfield star Steve Murray turns to celebrate McNeill's misfortune .

Goalkeeper Bobby Clark (1965-1980) joined Aberdeen from Eddie Turnbull's old club Queen's Park in May 1965. Son of a Clyde director who became Treasurer of the SFA, Bobby stood between the posts at Pittodrie for fifteen years and collected a League Championship medal in his 'swansong' season of 1979/80. Capped on seventeen occasions for Scotland, Clark made a total of 593 competitive appearances for Aberdeen and won all the domestic and international honours on offer.

Custodian Ernie McGarr played only fifty-eight games as Aberdeen's last-line, around 1969-1970, but managed to make two Scotland appearances in that time against Austria and Eire. He returned to being Bobby Clark's understudy in 1970, later starring at Dunfermline, East Fife, Cowdenbeath, Airdrie and Berwick Rangers.

Bobby Clark makes a save against Celtic at Parkhead in the 1972/73 season.

Midfield maestro Steve Murray was born in Dumbarton on 9 October 1944, joining Dundee from local team St Patrick's in 1963. He cost the Dons a record fee of £50,000 in March 1970 and went on to make 140 competitive appearances. Murray was transferred to Celtic in 1973 for £50,000, and later managed Forfar Athletic for three days in 1980. An accountant by profession and a published caricaturist, he subsequently served Dundee United as reserve team coach.

Zoltan Varga signed from Hertha Berlin in October 1972, making 31 competitive appearances and scoring 10 goals for Aberdeen during his only season (1972/73) at Pittodrie. Hungarian international and star forward Varga helped Ferencvaros reach the Fairs Cup final of 1968, winning his country's Player of the Year award that same year. A magical footballer, he simply mesmerised opponents with his brilliant ball control, dribbling skills and perfect passing ability. In 1973 Varga moved to European Cup holders Ajax.

Alex Willoughby (1969–1974) cost Aberdeen £25,000 from Rangers on 31 May 1969. He made 150appearances for the Dons plus 28 as sub, and was appointed player/coach at Pittodrie before moving to Hong Kong where he teamed up with his cousin, Jim Forrest. An outgoing personality, Willoughby was a public relations officer at Ibrox in the 1990s. At the age of 59, he sadly passed away in July 2004, following a battle with cancer.

Full-back Jim Hermiston (1965-1975) played 272 competitive games for Aberdeen. He signed from junior side Bonnyrigg Rose in 1965 and gave the Dons a decade of reliable service before retiring to join the police force. Hermiston later resumed his football career in Australia.

At the tender age of seventeen, Arthur Graham (1969-1977) played in Aberdeen's 1970 Scottish Cup final victory over Celtic. A direct outside left with a ferocious shot, Graham was born in Castlemilk, Glasgow on 26 October 1952, arriving in the Granite City from Cambuslang Rangers during the 1969/1970 season. He signed for Leeds United in a £125,000 deal in July 1977 and moved to Manchester United for £45,000 in August 1983. He was csapped on ten occasions for Scotland.

Attacker Drew Jarvie (1979-1982) joined Aberdeen from Airdrieonians for £76,000 in May 1972. Drew scored many important goals for the Dons during his decade at Pittodrie, including the equalizer in the 1976/77 League Cup Final win over Celtic. In 1982 he moved back to Airdrie and was transferred to St Mirren the following year. Jarvie won three caps as a substitute for Scotland in 1971.